BIBLE EXPOSITION SERIES

HEBREWS: CHRIST IS SUPERIOR

NATHAN S. WHITLEY

Bible Exposition Series

Hebrews: Christ is Superior

Cover Design: Isaiah Comer/Comer Creative

Studying and teaching the Bible is one of my greatest joys. The Lord Jesus Christ has graced me with many opportunities to do that throughout my ministry. A couple of years ago, Rob Akers, Pastor of Landmark Apostolic Church in Bloomington, Indiana, asked me to teach through a New Testament letter for their Bread of Life Bible Conference. I have had the honor of being able to do that for the last two years.

In 2021, I taught the Hebrews letter. This book is the fruit of that study and teaching. While this isn't a verse-by-verse exposition, it does offer an introduction to Hebrews and an overview of each section and chapter. I have included study guides with questions to help students better internalize the contents of Hebrews.

A fruitful method of Bible study is reading and studying a single book of the Bible repeatedly. I would encourage you to do just that with Hebrews while using this book as a guide.

Nathan S. Whitley

Knoxville, Tennessee

BIBLE EXPOSITION SERIES
HEBREWS: CHRIST IS SUPERIOR

Hebrews Outline

1. **Jesus the Superior Person (Hebrews 1-6)**

A. Superior to the Prophets (1:1-3)
B. Superior to the Angels (1:4-2:18)
C. Superior to Moses (3:1-4:13)
D. Superior to Aaron (4:14-6:20)

2. **Jesus the Superior Priest (Hebrews 7-10)**

A. Superior Order (7:1-28)
B. Superior Covenant (8:1-13)
C. Superior Tabernacle (9:1-28)
D. Superior Sacrifice (10:1-39)

3. **Jesus the Superior Principle (Hebrews 11-13)**

A. Superior Faith (11:1-40)
B. Superior Endurance (12:1-29)
C. Exhortations and Conclusion (13:1-25)

Five Warnings

A. Drifting from the Word of God (Heb. 2:1-4)
B. Doubting the Word of God (Heb. 3:7-4:13)
C. Dullness of Hearing the Word of God (Heb. 5:11-6:20)
D. Despising the Word of God (Heb. 10:26-29)
E. Denying the Word of God (Heb. 12:14-29)

Who Wrote Hebrews?

Throughout history, many writers have been considered as the writer of Hebrews. Here are a few of the more popular suggestions.

Paul

Similarities in vocabulary identify Hebrews as a Pauline work. However, the numerous words unique to Hebrews could argue against Pauline authorship. The reference to Timothy (13:23) is a mark of Pauline authorship (Rom. 16:21, 1 Cor. 4:17; Phil 1:1; 1 Thess.

3:2). Likewise, Timothy would have been close to numerous people due to his work in Philippi (Phil. 2:19–24); Thessalonica (1 Thess. 3:1–10), Corinth (1 Cor. 4:17, 16:10–11), and Asia Minor (Acts 19:22; 1 Tim 1:3). The Hebrews letter lacks a greeting and salutation, whereas Paul always introduced himself in his letters.

Since Jewish audiences rejected Paul and his ministry (Acts 13:46; 18:6), some have argued that he left his name out to gain acceptance. While that might seem plausible, such an argument is purely conjecture. Nowhere in the New Testament do we find Paul ever avoiding controversy. Furthermore, the Lord told Paul not to be afraid of anyone and continue preaching the gospel (Acts 18:9-11).

Barnabas

Barnabas befriended Paul after his conversion and helped dismiss suspicions concerning the genuineness of Paul's confession of faith in Christ (Acts 9:26–28). Apparently, Barnabas was not as eloquent a speaker as Paul (Acts 14:12), so how could he have written an effective rhetorical letter like Hebrews?

Apollos

Scripture records Apollos was "mighty" or "well-versed" in the Scriptures (Acts 18:24, 28), and the author of Hebrews was undoubtedly well-versed in the Old Testament. Furthermore, Apollos was an educated man and a great orator (Acts 18:24, 26, 28). The author of Hebrews employs a well-developed form of rhetoric, leading one to believe Apollos is the author of Hebrews.

Luke

Luke receives his information from others (Luke 1:1–4), as does the author of Hebrews (2:3). Luke was a companion and co-worker of Paul and aware of Jewish manners and customs. If a Gentile, would Jewish recipients be receptive to Luke's criticism of Old Testament commands and rites?

Unknown

For reasons unknown to us, the Hebrews writer failed to identify himself and his audience. The most practical purpose could be the recipients were familiar with the writer, and such salutation was unnecessary. It is probably in the best interest of Bible students to claim ignorance as to who wrote Hebrews.

INTRODUCTION TO HEBREWS

The Hebrews letter is one of the most intriguing books of the Bible. Many New Testament readers unfamiliar with the Old Testament may find its contents puzzling or irrelevant. However, Hebrews reveals the Bible is not a collection of unrelated stories but a unified story - the story of humanity's redemption through Jesus Christ. Hebrews unfolds the glorious tapestry of God's progressive revelation and its climax in Jesus, allowing us to see His superiority.

Hebrews is an excellent aid in seeing Jesus Christ throughout the Old Testament. For instance, there are at least 35 direct quotations from the Old Testament, along with numerous allusions and references. Hebrews is one of the most Jewish books in the New Testament and does at least three things for Christian believers. First, Hebrews is a New Testament commentary on the Old Testament illuminating integral Jewish themes. Old Testament rituals, prophecies, and people are more than just critical historical matters; they point to Israel's long-awaited Messiah, Jesus.

Second, Hebrews is a beautiful example of how New Testament believers interpreted the Old Testament using a particular Jesus hermeneutic. Suppose Scripture doesn't teach us a proper hermeneutic by showing how the biblical authors interpreted other biblical texts. In that case, we would bring an external system to Scripture that displaces the authority of Scripture. As we see in Hebrews, the New Testament authors correctly used and interpreted the Old Testament. First Century believers didn't disregard the Old Testament in favor of the New Testament, for there wasn't yet a New Testament compiled. Consequently, they relied heavily upon the Old Testament to point to Jesus's person and work.

Third, Hebrews teaches that Jesus Christ is the ultimate revelation of God. Through the person and work of Jesus Christ, redemption from sin is made possible.

Writer

Unlike other New Testament epistles, Hebrews does not identify its writer. Debates have raged throughout Christian history as to who may have written this fantastic letter. Scholars have proposed the following people as potential writers: Paul, Barnabas, Luke, Apollos, Clement of Rome, and others. (For a closer look at some of these potential writers, please see page six.)

The writer must have been a second-generation Christian, for he said of the gospel message, "It was declared at first by the Lord, and it was attested to us by those who heard" (Heb. 2:3). Such insight potentially rules out Paul, who claimed to have received revelation directly from the Lord Jesus (1 Cor. 15:8; Gal. 1:12). However, the writer of Hebrews had a personal relationship with Timothy (Heb. 13:23). While Paul claimed Timothy to be his son in the faith (1 Tim. 1:2), this doesn't necessarily make him the writer of Hebrews, for many of the believers of the first century knew Timothy (Acts 19:22; 1 Cor. 4:17, 16:10; 1 Thess. 3:2,6).

Origen, considered an early Church Father, wrote, "But as to who wrote the epistle of Hebrews, God knows the truth of the matter." Agreeing with Origen seems to be the most logical of answers concerning the writer of Hebrews.

Audience

Not only do we have uncertainty as to who wrote Hebrews, but the letter also doesn't reveal the exact audience either. The title "To the Hebrews," found in most Bibles, was added in the second century but wasn't part of the original text. Early Christians likely entitled it Hebrews due to the amount of Old Testament content it contains.

There are certain clues that we can study to reach a reasonable conclusion as to who the writer was addressing. First, the writer's usage of Old Testament references leads the reader to believe the audience must have been Jewish. Additionally, he considered the patriarchs and prophets to be their forefathers (Heb. 1:1). Next, the writer was confident of their confession of faith in Jesus Christ (Heb. 3:1), and he considered them to be "brothers" and "dear friends" (Heb. 3:12, 6:9, 7:5, 10:19, 13:22). All of this leads us to conclude the audience must have been Jewish Christians.

Again, we are without clear information as to the location of the author or the audience. There seems to be some evidence concluding the letter: "Greet all your leaders and all the saints. Those who come from Italy send you greetings" (13:24). Did the writer pen the letter from Italy? Or did he write to believers in Italy? Once again, we have to lean upon what evidence we have and reach a reasonable conclusion. Most Bible commentators, however, seem to believe the writer was addressing Jewish Christians in Rome.

Genre

Hebrews isn't a letter like Romans or Galatians. Instead, it's a word of exhortation, for the writer says, "I appeal to you, brothers, bear with my word of exhortation, for I have written to you briefly" (Hebrews 13:22). The Greek word for "exhortation" refers to a synagogue homily or sermon. In other words, Hebrews is more of a sermon than it is a letter.

The structure even lends itself to a sermon rather than a letter. Unlike other New Testament letters (epistles), it lacks the typical pleasantries of greetings. The writer instead jumps right into his sermon. We may call it a sermon letter since it was written and sent like a letter.

Hebrews is a pastor's appeal to his people, and like most sermons, the writer has peppered his exposition with warnings and encouragement.

The Purpose of the Letter

The writer of Hebrews was addressing Jewish Christians who had left Judaism and, as a result, had suffered for the sake of the gospel of Jesus Christ (Heb. 10:32-34). The writer calls them to endure and hold fast to their faith in Jesus Christ in the face of such persecution. The writer implores his readers not to forsake the truth of Christ's person and work to return to the more comfortable rites of Judaism. From the text, we can also conclude the letter was written before the Temple's destruction in A.D. 70. The writer's use of the present tense when discussing sacrifices leads us to assume the Temple in Jerusalem was still erect (7:8; 9:6-7,13, 10:1-2; 13:10).

Considering these Christians may have been second-generation believers (Heb. 2:3), their lack of maturity may have also contributed to their retreat back to Judaism. The writer calls them to not only perseverance but also maturity. It's one thing to be weak in faith but failing to mature is something different altogether. As we will see early in our study, there's a difference between drifting carelessly away from the faith (Heb. 2) and rejecting it altogether. This is a matter of spiritual maturity and immaturity.

As we mentioned above, the writer desired to encourage these believers to persevere in the face of persecution. At some point in their Christian walk, they had suffered persecution. The writer records they had a hard struggle with suffering, were publicly exposed to reproach and afflictions, imprisoned, and even having their property confiscated (10:32-34). Due to such tribulation, some Jewish believers may have felt it safer to return to Judaism. The familiarity and comforts of their former belief system may have been enticing.

All these troubles and temptations may have led the Hebrews writer to encourage these particular believers. To prevent a people from forsaking the truth of God's Word, the writer had to appeal to their Jewish sensibilities and present Christ as the fulfillment of every vital landmark in the Old Testament.

Theme

The key theme throughout Hebrews is the superiority of Jesus. Simply put, Jesus is better. The writer develops his argument by contrasting Christ with several articles from the Old Testament. The writer makes clear that Jesus is the substance of what were mere shadows in the Old Testament (Heb. 8:5; 10:1; also see Col. 2:17)

The writer presents Christ as superior from the beginning to the end of the letter. He is superior to the prophets (1:1-3). He is superior to angels (1:4-2:18). He is superior to Moses (3:1-19). He is superior to Aaron and Melchizedek (5:14-7:28). He is superior to Judaism (8:1-10:39). He is superior to Old Testament saints (11:1-12:3).

The writer of Hebrews aims to present Jesus, and consequently faith in Jesus, as a superior form of belief. The writer doesn't undermine the Old Testament's patriarchs, prophets, or principles; instead, he seeks to let his readers know that everything in the Old Testament was pointing towards a greater realization in Jesus.

Hebrews Relevance Today

While you may not face the temptation to go back to Judaism and offer animal sacrifices or closely follow the ceremonial and civil laws of the Mosaic covenant, you might have the temptation, however, to leave Christianity for the things of this world. You may not like the idea of facing tribulation and persecution, so you may want to find a more accessible or more acceptable form of religion. And, as we will see, the Hebrews weren't tempted by such apostasy overnight. Instead, it was the slow drift of forsaking Jesus. Likewise, we may not be tempted to leave our faith in Jesus overnight, but over time we may drift from our first love. We may lose sight of Jesus' superiority over all other religions and ways of life.

Hebrews is also a relevant call for believers to mature in their faith. Does this New Testament book have some problematic passages? Certainly. Do Hebrews include some strong warnings? Absolutely. Does this word of exhortation involve many unfamiliar Old Testament themes? Yes. But at some point, as a Christian, you will have to forsake the shallow end of faith and wade out into the depths of truth. While some truths could be considered difficult to understand, these heavenly realities will help you mature and preserve your faith, proving Christ is superior not only to all other religions, but He is also superior to every trial and tribulation we may face.

Introduction to Hebrews Questions

Who are some proposed writers of Hebrews?

____

____

____

Paul is a potential writer of Hebrews. From the text, what are some arguments against Pauline authorship?

____

____

____

Who was the Hebrews writer addressing?

____

____

____

Hebrews isn't like other New Testament letters. The structure lends itself to a ____________________ rather than a letter.

____

____

____

What is the key theme of Hebrews?

____

____

____

According to the writer, everything in the Old Testament was pointing to whom?

____

____

____

Hebrews is relevant to believers in what ways?

____

____

____

Introduction to Hebrews Notes

HEBREWS EXPOSITION

SECTION ONE:
JESUS THE SUPERIOR PERSON (HEBREWS 1-6)

Superior to the Prophets (1:1-3)

Superior to the Angels (1:4-2:18)

Superior to Moses (3:1-4:13)

Superior to Aaron (4:14-6:20)

Superior to the Prophets (1:1-3)

Hebrews opens with a bang. No introduction, no greeting, or pleasantries. It simply begins with the declaration that God has spoken. It has a similar feel to the opening of Genesis, where the reader is abruptly introduced to a creating and speaking God. Similarly, Hebrews flings the door wide open and says God has spoken. And it's true, throughout redemptive history, God has spoken. He spoke through prophets like Moses, David, and Elijah. Men like these and others were heralds of God's truth and story. They spoke on behalf of God, employing various methods of communication such as parables, visions, dreams, and even poetry.

The ultimate expression of God's revelation, however, is Jesus Christ, the Son of God. Jesus is the complete revelation of God's Word. The Apostle John wrote, "In the beginning was the Word, and the Word was with God, and the Word was God. And the Word became flesh and dwelt among us, and we have seen his glory, glory as of the only Son from the Father, full of grace and truth" (John 1:1,14). Jesus is the Word of God in flesh and blood. He is the express image of the invisible God (Col. 1:15; Heb. 1:3).

The Word of God in the Old Testament held great weight and demanded obedience. Consequently, failure to obey the message of the prophets meant divine punishment. Now the Son of God is God's final Word. To be obedient to Jesus Christ brings life; to reject Him and His Word is death. The Hebrews writer thus clarifies - obey the Son of God through faith, and do not disobey Him, because His word is far superior to that of the prophets. The Hebrews writer sets out to make evident having faith in Jesus, the Word of God, is the supreme principle of life. Choosing to have confidence in Christ fuels obedience and perseverance.

The first three verses are the writer's thesis. For the rest of the exhortation, he proves his thesis by contrasting Jesus with various prophets, priests, and kings who spoke on behalf of God. As we will see, Jesus is superior to prophets like Moses. He is superior to angels who mediated the Law of Moses. Jesus is superior to priests such as the Levites. And finally, Jesus is superior to kings like Melchizedek. What sets Jesus apart from the prophets, angels, priests, and kings of the Old Testament is that He gave His life for the salvation of others: "After making purification for sins, he sat down at the right hand of the Majesty on high" (1:3).

Superior to the Prophets Study Guide (1:1-3)

The Hebrews writer begins with declaring that God has
____.

____

____

____

God has spoken throughout history. In what ways has God spoken?

____

____

____

Jesus is superior to prophets. Name some prophets from the Old Testament.

____

____

____

God's final Word to humanity is what?

____

____

____

Superior to the Angels (1:4-2:18)

Similar to Paul's rebuke of worshiping angels in Colossians (Col. 2:18), the writer's following argument proves Christ's superiority over angels. The distinguishing mark that sets Jesus apart from the angels is making the purification of sin possible. Angels are ministering spirits, and spirits do not have flesh and blood, meaning this would make it impossible for an angel to atone for the sins of humanity. God needed to robe Himself in the flesh so He could offer a blood offering to save the world. As we will see in Hebrews 12, the blood of Jesus is superior to all other blood because it was the very blood of God (Acts 20:28).

That truth alone should be sufficient to show Jesus's superiority over angels. The writer continues, however, declaring the Son to have a name more excellent than angels. The Name of the Son of God isn't Son; it is Jesus. When the Son of God came into the world, he was given a name: Jesus. The angel declared to Mary and Joseph, "You shall call his name Jesus, for he will save his people from their sins" (Matt. 1:21). The name Jesus means Jehovah-Saves.

Jesus was not another lord nor another god. Instead, Jesus was God incarnate, revealing the only Name that can save (Acts 4:12). Additionally, Jesus was the manifest presence of Yahweh (the covenant name of Israel's God), for he was called "Immanuel," meaning God with us (Matt. 1:23). The Name of Jesus didn't replace Yahweh, rather Jesus came in the Name of Yahweh (Pss. 118:26; Matt. 23:29; Jn. 5:43; Heb. 1:4), and the name Jesus was given to Him through inheritance (Heb. 1:4).

A son receives an inheritance from his father. Though angels could be considered "sons of God" (Job 1:6; 38:7), they were not the Son of God. Likewise, angels are created, and the Son of God was begotten. Meaning the Son was not created as in He was lesser than God. Instead, the Son of God was God. As God, the Son made all things. He wasn't God's assistant in creation. No, He was the very agent of creation. As God, He was above the angels, but in the incarnation (that is, robing Himself in flesh and blood), he subjected Himself to humanity. This is a paradox. As God was in the body of Jesus Christ, He didn't cease to be God. Christ's Sonship began in the virgin's womb. Before Sonship, he was the Word or "Logos" of God. Jesus is the Father incarnate because He is the Word incarnate–and the Word is the express image of the Father. Furthermore, the Word is ontologically Father because the Word is God and the Father is the Only True God.

The writer also adds that angels are merely servants of God. Jesus, on the other hand, His Son. Through inheritance, Jesus's kingly authority makes everything subject to Him. The paradox continues in that everything is subject to Jesus, yet He subjected Himself to suffering and death on behalf of humanity (2:8-10). He does this because humanity has been subjected to sin and death, becoming our merciful and faithful High Priest (2:15-16). The result of Christ's suffering is the liberation of humanity from sin, sanctifying them and bringing them into the family of God. Jesus was crowned with glory and honor through this suffering. Likewise, as sinners are adopted into the family of God, they subject themselves to suffering, becoming fellow-heirs with Christ so that they might be glorified with Him (Rom. 8:17).

Finally, angels are inferior to Christ, living in subjection to Christ's rule and reign. Furthermore, they cannot procure humanity's salvation because they do not have flesh and blood - that which was needed to provide salvation (Heb. 9:22). And finally, it was not angels that Christ came to redeem; that glorious reality was given to sinful humanity. This glorious salvation is what angels long to look into (1 Peter 1:12).

Superior to the Angels Study Guide (1:4-2:18)

What is the distinguishing mark that sets Jesus apart from angels?

____

____

____

What is the name of the Son of God? Which New Testament texts provide the answer?

____

____

____

When did Christ's sonship begin?

____

____

____

Jesus Christ's blood is superior because it is the very blood of ______________________________.

____

____

____

Warning One: Drifting from the Word of God (2:1-4)

Strategically throughout the letter, the writer warns his readers. Many opinions are available concerning these warnings. For example, some question the authenticity of the believer's conversion. Others consider whether or not believers can lose their salvation. These are valid concerns. Readers must be cautious not to wrestle these warnings away from their context; this is why we always keep the audience and the writer's theme in mind as we study Biblical texts.

As seen from the introduction, the writer's audience was Jewish Christians tempted to return to Judaism when faced with suffering and tribulation. They also lacked in spiritual maturity. This audience of Jewish Christians needed to realize that Jesus Christ was superior to all that Judaism had to offer.

With this in mind, chapter two introduces the first of five warnings in Hebrews. The first warning is to avoid drifting from the Word of God: "Therefore we must pay much closer attention to what we have heard, lest we drift away from it" (2:1). The writer urges his audience to pay closer attention to what they have heard, which was the gospel of Jesus Christ.

Looking back to the inauguration of the Law of Moses at Mt. Sinai, a host of angels accompanied the Lord: "The Lord came from Sinai and dawned from Seir upon us; he shone forth from Mount Paran; he came from the ten thousands of holy ones, with flaming fire at his right hand" (Deut. 33:2). In his final sermon, Stephen mentioned an angel was with Moses in the mountain, and angels delivered the Law (Acts 7:38, 53).

Moreover, great signs and wonders accompanied the inauguration of the Law at Mt. Sinai: "Now when all the people saw the thunder and the flashes of lightning and the sound of the trumpet and the mountain smoking, the people were afraid and trembled, and they stood far off" (Ex. 20:18). The reason for this dramatic display of God's power was to incite fear and obedience. The gospel of Jesus Christ was declared in similar ways to that of the Law at Mt. Sinai. The writer said, "how shall we escape if we neglect such a great salvation? It was declared at first by the Lord, and it was attested to us by those who heard, while God also bore witness by signs and wonders and various miracles and by gifts of the Holy Spirit distributed according to his will" (2:3-4).

Therefore, the writer warns, "How shall we escape if we neglect such a great salvation?" If the Law of Moses demanded punishment for every transgression, how much more should we take heed to the gospel? Jesus is far superior to angels and Moses. The phrase "pay much closer attention" in Greek means to hold onto with earnestness. The reason for holding onto the truth of the gospel? The writer answers: "lest we drift away from it." The Greek phrase "to drift away" has several meanings. It could refer to something floating by in the water or to a ring carelessly slipping off a finger. Putting the two phrases together, we can see the warning: to prevent from carelessly drifting away, earnestly hold onto the Word of God.

Contrary to popular opinion, believers don't deliberately backslide; instead, they drift away carelessly, neglecting the truth they once held dear. Drifting can take place in the daily decisions of life. It's the neglecting of prayer and reading God's Word. It's the attitude of apathy that leads to disregarding corporate worship and Christian fellowship. Beloved, in times of tribulation and in times of peace, it is necessary to hold onto the Word of God.

Warning One: Drifting from the Word of God Study Guide (2:1-4)

The phrase "pay much closer attention" in Greek means what?

____

____

____

What's the reasoning for holding onto the truth of the gospel?

____

____

____

How can believers drift away from the truth of God's Word?

____

____

____

Superior to Moses (3:1-4:13)

The writer declares Jesus to be the Apostle and High Priest of our faith. The word "apostle" means one sent with a message on behalf of another. An example of this is when the Father sending Jesus into the world so sinful humanity might have life through him (1 Jn. 4:9). Part of Jesus' mission was revealing God the Father, who any man had never seen. Jesus entered the world as the Father's perfect representative because Jesus and the Father are one (Jn. 10:30; 17:11, 21, 23). Since the Father and the Son are one, Jesus can thereby perfectly reveal God (Jn. 1:18). The Son of God accomplished the works of the Father (Jn. 10:37-39).

Furthermore, Jesus spoke with the authority of the Father (Jn. 12:49-50). The Father was also a witness to who Jesus was and to the works that He did (Jn. 5:36-37). Therefore, Jesus was the quintessential Apostle sent to represent and reveal the Words and works of God. The same type of representative ministry is seen throughout the New Testament with the apostles and continues with New Testament believers, our heavenly calling (Mk. 16:17-20; Jn. 14:12).

In addition to being our Apostle, Jesus is our High Priest. The writer unpacks the priestly duties of Christ in greater depth in later chapters; we should note that a high priest was a mediator between God and humanity. Jesus did this perfectly.

Taking these two roles into consideration, Jesus is greater than Moses, who was also sent on behalf of God and functioned as a mediator of God's message to Israel (3:5). Moses performed his calling with faithfulness. Just as

Moses led Israel out of Egypt's bondage into freedom and God's covenant, Jesus liberated humanity from sin's bondage and meditated a new and better covenant.

Moses faithfully served Israel, the house of God, as a servant (3:3). Jesus faithfully oversees the Church, God's new house, as a Son (3:3-4). This new house of God is twofold. First, individual believers are considered the house of God (1 Cor. 3:9; 6:15-20). Second, the house of God is the gathered body of believers (Eph. 2:19-20).

Superior to Moses Study Guide (3:1-4:13)

Moses served God's house as a what?

____

____

____

Jesus serves God's house as a what?

____

____

____

In what two ways can the house of God be described today?

____

____

____

Warning Two: Doubting the Word of God (3:7-4:13)

"Therefore, as the Holy Spirit says, 'Today, if you hear his voice, do not harden your hearts as in the rebellion, on the day of testing in the wilderness.'" The writer's use of "therefore" should alert Bible students. Therefore means "because of that" or "in consequence of that." Because Jesus is our Apostle and High Priest and serves as a Son over the house of God, we should not harden our hearts. The writer's second warning is a cautioning of hardening one's heart. To drive home his point, the writer refers to Israel's time wandering in the wilderness.

Hebrews 3:7-11 is a quotation from Psalm 95. The first half of Psalm 95 is a call to worship God (Ps. 95:1-7). The second half of the psalm looks back at Israel's unbelief in the wilderness (Ps. 95:8-11). The events of Psalm 95 are found in Exodus 17 and Numbers 14. The first account is Israel's murmuring for water, in which Moses struck a rock with his staff and forthwith came water (Ex.17:5-7). Massah and Meribah, the name of that place, means rebellion and contention. The second account is Israel's refusal to conquer Canaan and seize the Promised Land (Num. 14:1-5). Israel provoked the Lord with their disobedience, causing them to wander for forty years. Their hard hearts drew this indicting statement: "they saw my works, yet they have not known my ways" (3:9-10 author's translation).

Unbelief is an overlooked sin. In the biblical sense, unbelief is the failure to believe and adhere to the Word of God. Israel's unbelief in the wilderness caused an entire generation to miss out on the Promised Land. This unbelief was a fatal refusal of God's Word. The writer warns his readers to hear the gospel message of Jesus Christ today. In like manner, the writer is warning his readers not to harden their hearts.

Israel received several signs of God's faithfulness and provision, yet they still refused to believe. New Testament believers have received an even greater symbol of God's faithfulness and provision, and that is the life, death, and resurrection of Jesus Christ. This heavenly provision brings more than the rest of Canaan, and this is eternal rest.

Beloved, the Word of God is a powerful weapon (4:12). This Sword of the Spirit (Eph. 6:17) can cut through any heart hardened with doubt. In an age where doubt has become the norm, allow the Word of God to soften your heart towards faith in Jesus Christ.

Warning Two: Doubting the Word of God Study Guide (3:7-4:13)

The second warning to believers includes not hardening your heart. The writer illustrates his point by using what example from the Old Testament?

What happened at Massah and Meribah (Exodus 17:5-7; Numbers 14:1-5)?

New Testament believers have received a more significant symbol of God's faithfulness and provision. What is it?

Superior to Aaron (4:14-6:20)

Next, the writer shifts to revealing Christ's superior priesthood. Aaron, Moses's brother, was Israel's first high priest. Jesus is considered a Great High Priest (4:14). There were two qualifications to be a priest. First, he had to be a human, for he had to act on behalf of men in relation to God (5:1). The priest's humanity enabled him to deal gently with the weakness of others (5:2). Second, God appointed the priest. No one was to take this calling upon himself (5:4). Israel's history recorded several men who attempted to do priestly work without the appointment of God, and it ended tragically. The earth swallowed up Korah as he and his tribe tried to usurp the Levite's duties. King Saul was stripped of the throne when offered sacrifices without permission. Lastly, King Uzziah was struck with leprosy as he ventured to offer sacrifices.

Christ meets both of these qualifications. He was entirely God and fully human. The writer notes that Jesus was a real man with flesh, emotions, and feelings (5:7-8). Jesus was also called of God to be a high priest (5:10). It was important for Jesus to be a man and appointed of God, for this allowed Him to sympathize with sinner's weaknesses and understand their temptations (5:15). Christ's understanding of humanity's frailties gives believers confidence to draw near to the throne of grace that we may receive mercy and find grace to help in time of need (5:16).

Eight Keys Christ's Priesthood Provides

1. He understands our weaknesses
2. He gives us access to the throne of God
3. He deals gently with us
4. He became the source of eternal life
5. He is a mediator of a better covenant
6. He perfects us
7. He intercedes on our behalf
8. He takes away sin once and for all

Superior to Aaron Study Guide (4:14-6:20)

What were the two qualifications to be a Levitical priest? How does Jesus meet those two qualifications?

____

____

____

Jesus' humanity allows Him to relate to sinful humanity. How does that encourage believers?

____

____

____

What are some ways Christ's priesthood is superior to that of Aaron's?

____

____

____

Warning Three: Departing from the Word of God (5:11-6:20)

The third warning is to avoid departing from the Word of God and dulling our senses to the Word of God. The Hebrews weren't maturing spiritually. Their lack of maturity kept them on a diet of spiritual milk. When they should have been teaching, they were still in need of being taught fundamental truths. He contrasts their childish diet with that of those who have matured into digesting the strong meat of God's Word (5:11-13). Having a steady diet of solid truth yields a greater discernment between good and evil (5:14). These Jewish Christians needed to know more than the basics and grow into maturity, or the consequence would be to fall away (6:4-8).

The writer gives six foundational teachings that his readers should be comfortable knowing and moving on from.

- Faith
- Repentance
- Baptisms (washings)
- Laying on of hands
- Resurrection from the dead
- Eternal judgment

All these foundational doctrines have their parallels within the Old and New Testaments. And indeed, all of these doctrines are important and necessary. Additionally, the writer isn't suggesting not teaching these doctrines. The issue didn't lie within the doctrines. The problem was having to teach these truths repeatedly to this particular audience. To the writer, this repetitious teaching of fundamental truths was a sign of immaturity. Such immaturity could undoubtedly lead to departing from the Word of God. The writer warns: "For it is impossible, in the case of those who have once been enlightened, who have tasted the heavenly gift, and have shared in the Holy Spirit...and then have fallen away, to restore them again to repentance.." (6:4-6). Notice the three words "enlightened," "tasted," and "shared." These words do not necessarily describe New Testament salvation, at least not in their entirety. New Testament words for salvation include being born again (Jn. 3:3), salvation (Rom. 1:16), justification (Rom. 5:18), redemption (Rom. 3:23-24), faith and righteousness (Rom. 1:17). If one has been enlightened and tasted heavenly gifts and departs from them, they are in danger. Where can they turn in faith and repentance? They will not turn to Christ because they do not believe Him to be true. If they turn back to Judaism, they know it to be inferior to Christ, for they have been "enlightened" and "tasted" that which is authentic.

Beloved, this isn't a matter of a believer sinning and never finding forgiveness. Instead, this is a complete rejection of Christ and the Word of God. They do not want to repent of their sins, for they openly reject God's truth after knowing it. The Christian who sins has a promise for the Apostle John wrote, "If we confess our sins, he is faithful and just to forgive us our sins and to cleanse us from all unrighteousness" (1 Jn. 1:9). The great apostle included himself in that "we" statement, certainly giving hope for all those not considered apostles who daily wage war against their sinful flesh.

Someone has said, "Christ offers hope for the fallen, but cannot offer anything to the fallen away."

The writer reveals the heart of a pastor: "Though we speak in this way, yet in your case, beloved, we feel sure of better things - things that belong to salvation" (Heb. 6:9). Many pastors ache when giving their congregation a dose of hard truth, so they quickly apply the salve of grace. The writer wants to assure them God hasn't overlooked their labor of serving one another in love (6:10-11).

Four Marks of the Mature Christian

1. Discern good from evil (5:14)
2. Doctrinal understanding (5:11-13)
3. Serving one another (6:9-12)
4. Faithfulness (6:18-19)

The believer needs assurance. One thing they can be sure of is God's character and nature. There are two things God can't do. First, He cannot change, meaning He is immutable (Mal. 3:6). He is the same yesterday, today, and forever (Heb. 13:8). The second thing God can't do is lie. That which God spoke formerly and that which He speaks today and tomorrow will not vary in any manner. The Hebrews weren't to take refuge in their faithfulness. Instead, they were to take refuge in God's faithfulness: "We have this as a sure and steadfast anchor of the soul, a hope that enters into the inner place behind the curtain, where Jesus has gone as a forerunner on our behalf, having become a high priest forever after the order of Melchizedek" (Heb. 6:19-20).

Warning Three: Departing from the Word of God Study Guide (5:11-6:20)

What are the six foundational teachings that the Hebrews readers should be comfortable knowing?

Is the writer suggesting not teaching these foundational teachings? If not, what is he suggesting?

The Jewish Christian's constant need to be taught these teachings was a sign of what?

The words "enlightened," "tasted," and "shared" do not necessarily describe New Testament salvation. What New Testament words and phrases describe salvation?

What are the four marks of the mature Christian?

____

____

____

Jesus the Superior Person Notes

SECTION TWO:
JESUS THE SUPERIOR PRIEST (HEBREWS 7-10)

Superior Order (7:1-28)

Superior Covenant (8:1-13)

Superior Tabernacle (9:1-28)

Superior Sacrifice (10:1-39)

Superior Order (7:1-8:5)

The Hebrews writer begins to give his audience some solid theological food. He started this discourse on Melchizedek just before his third warning (5:10). Here in chapter seven, he picks up where he left off.

The mysterious figure Melchizedek is introduced in Genesis after Abraham rescues Lot (Gen. 14:18-24). He's mentioned again in Psalm 110, which is the most quoted psalm in the New Testament. Psalm 110 is full of messianic imagery, which makes the reference to Melchizedek even more intriguing. (For more insight into Melchizedek, read The King's Bread and Wine).

Five Ways Christ's Priesthood is Superior

1. Jesus didn't come from the priestly tribe of Levi. Instead, He descended from the kingly tribe of Judah (Gen. 49:10; Heb. 7:14).

2. Christ is eternal, meaning His priesthood lives on forever (7:16, 24). The Levites, on the other hand, were mortal and were subject to death (7:23).

3. The Levitical priesthood was insufficient. The Law and its sacrifices could not perfect anything (7:11,18-19). Christ, on the other hand, can save to the uttermost (7:25).

4. Because of their sinful nature, the Levitical priests had to offer sacrifices for themselves first, then offer sacrifices on behalf of others (7:27). Jesus, our High Priest, is holy, innocent, unstained, and separated from sinners, does not need to offer sacrifices for

Himself. Instead, He offered up Himself as a sacrifice for all (7:26-28).

5. The Levitical priests served as mediators of an inferior covenant (8:6-7). Jesus, however, mediates a better covenant with better promises (8:6). The priesthood of Jesus offers a better hope with better promises. The better hope gives us access to God directly (7:19).

Believers no longer need an earthly priest to mediate on their behalf; through Christ, we can come boldly to the throne of grace to obtain mercy. Christ's all-sufficient sacrifice offers better promises. Promises such as believers sharing in Christ's vicarious victory.

Another promise includes Christ's heavenly intercession for us. According to the writer of Hebrews, Jesus sat down on the right hand of God to intercede on our behalf (1:3; 7:25). The "right hand" is a place of power and honor. Jesus doesn't use His kingly power for His own needs. Instead, He prays and intercedes on our account. Robert M'Cheyne said, "If I can hear Christ praying for me in the next room, I would not fear a million enemies. Yet the distance makes no difference; He is praying for me."

Superior Order Study Guide (7:1-8:5)

Why do New Testament believers no longer need an earthly priest?

When the Bible mentions God's right hand, what does that mean?

As Jesus functions in heaven as our High Priest, what is He doing presently?

Superior Covenant (8:6-13)

Christ's work as High Priest unveiled and initiated the new covenant. The old covenant (also known as the Law, the Law of Moses, Torah, or the Ten Commandments) revealed the people's faults (Rom. 7:7-11). The Law was perfect and good (Ps. 19:7; Rom. 7:12); unfortunately, it didn't make anyone perfect. The Law was conditional upon Israel's obedience, yet it lacked the vehicle for people to obey the commands, and it lacked any hope of inner change. Consequently, Israel continually broke the Law. Therefore, a new law had to be enacted - a law that could change hearts. The writer refers to Jeremiah's prophecy of a new covenant that would change hearts (Jer. 31:31-34; Heb. 8:10-13). With the new covenant (also known as the New Testament), the Holy Spirit empowers the believer to live by the Spirit (Rom. 8:3-4). Notice the repeated refrain of God's "I wills": "I will establish," "I will make," "I will put," "I will be their God," "I will be merciful," "I will remember their sins no more." The better covenant is not conditional upon humanity's frail will. Instead, God's love, grace, and mercy enacted this New Covenant.

The writer perfectly summarizes this glorious truth: "In speaking of a new covenant, he makes the first one obsolete. What is becoming obsolete and growing old is ready to vanish away." Beloved, let us rejoice over a better covenant with better hope and promises initiated through Jesus Christ, our High Priest!

Superior Covenant Study Guide (8:6-13)

The Law was perfect; it just couldn't perfect anyone. True or False?

___

___

___

What did the Law lack for the Israelites?

___

___

___

Human will did not enact the New Covenant. What enacted the New Covenant?

___

___

___

Superior Tabernacle (9:1-14)

The Tabernacle was the central place of worship during Israel's wanderings in the wilderness (Ex. 25:1-30:38). The Tabernacle would also serve as the blueprints for Solomon's temple in Jerusalem. The writer wants his readers to know that the ordinances of the Tabernacle foreshadowed Christ's sacrificial death. (For more insight into the Tabernacle and Jesus, read the article The Tabernacle of God).

Superior Sacrifice (9:15-10:39)

The ministry of the Old Testament priesthood took place at the Tabernacle. Priests were to perform specific tasks for specific sacrifices. The entire sacrificial system was strategic. Any deviation from the instructions would have dire consequences (Lev. 10:1-2).

Four Limitations of the Law's Sacrificial System

1. Only the high priest could enter the Holy of Holies (9:7).

2. Only enter the Holy of Holies once a year on the Day of Atonement (Lev. 23:26-27; 9:7,25).

3. Only with sacrificial blood of an animal could he enter the Holy of Holies (9:19).

4. Only efficacious for one year (10:3).

Christ's entrance into a heavenly Holy of Holies made without hands reveals Christ's superior priesthood (9:11,24). First, Christ shed His blood for sin (9:12a), then entered into that Holiest of places once and for all (10:10,12). Christ's sacrifice secured an eternal redemption (9:12b).

Four Ways Christ's Sacrifice is Superior

1. Animals are inferior to Christ, the Lamb of God (Jn. 1:36).

2. Animals were to be without blemish externally. Jesus is without blemish internally and externally (9:14).

3. Animals did not offer themselves; offerers chose them. Jesus willing offered Himself (9:25-28).

4. Animals could not take away sins (10:4,11). Christ's sacrifice obtained eternal redemption, purified our conscience, and sanctified us.

Those tempted to return to Judaism needed reminding of the inferiority of the Levitical priesthood. The Levitical priesthood was only limited to earthly ministry. And the seemingly endless train of livestock and the running river of blood from the Tabernacle's altar could never accomplish redemption.

Notice the position of Christ's heavenly ministry in contrast with the earthly ministry of the Levites: "And every priest stands daily at his service, repeatedly offering the same sacrifices, which can never take away sins. But when Christ had offered for all time a single sacrifice for sins, he sat down at the right hand of God" (10:11–12). The Levitical priests continually stood in the sanctuary, never sitting down. In essence, the Levitical priests never completed their duties. Those sacrifices were performed daily (7:27). Comparing that with Christ's perfect sacrifice of Himself, He offered it to God and sat down.

Bible commentator F.F. Bruce wrote, “A seated priest is the guarantee of a finished work and an acceptable sacrifice.” As noted earlier, Christ’s work of intercession on behalf of sinners is based on His perfect and efficacious sacrifice. Just as Jesus gave up the ghost, He cried out, “it is finished.” He was declaring His earthly work to be complete. In other words, there would no longer be any need for animal sacrifices or earthly tabernacles. The perfect Lamb of God had offered His righteous blood as the ultimate payment for sin’s debt. Now, in glory, Jesus is seated at the right hand of Majesty. Behold our enthroned High Priest!

Superior Tabernacle and Sacrifice Study Guide (9:1-14)

Where was the central place of worship during Israel's wilderness wanderings?

What were the four limitations of the Law's sacrificial system?

Once a year, the High Priest could enter into the Holy of Holies. What special day was it?

Name four ways the Levitical priesthood is inferior to Christ's priesthood.

What is the significance of the reference to the priest's standing and the sitting of Christ?

____

____

____

Warning Four: Despising the Word of God (10:26-29)

The fourth warning is quite similar to the third warning (5:11-6:20). The writer again refers to the demanding obedience of the Law of Moses. He quotes from Deuteronomy 17:2-7 to argue the severe consequences of rejecting the Law. This passage declares that those who despised the Lord's commands were put to death (10:28). He contrasts that with despising the gospel of Jesus Christ: "How much worse punishment, do you think, will be deserved by the one who has trampled underfoot the Son of God, and has profaned the blood of the covenant by which he was sanctified, and has outraged the Spirit of grace?" Concerning Jesus Christ's priesthood and sacrifice, the writer has made his point very clear: any attempt to return to Judaism would be futile. Any rejection of Christ's atoning work would result in a far severer punishment.

To sin willfully is to miss the mark. The greatest of sins is to reject Jesus Christ altogether. To reject Christ's superior Word, superior priesthood, and superior sacrifice is beyond the pale. Such rejection is to trample the Son of God under one's foot, to profane His blood, and to outrage the Spirit of Grace. Could this be the sin of blasphemy? Indeed, this seems to be the case. Some worry they may have blasphemed by accident. One cannot blaspheme out of ignorance. To blaspheme is to utterly and openly reject the person and work of Jesus Christ. There no longer remains a sacrifice of sins for such a person. The consequences for such a despising of the Word of God is a fearful expectation of eternal judgment and a fury of fire that will consume them (10:26-27,31).

This open rejection of Christ should strike fear into the heart of any believer. It is a terrifying thing to fall into the hands of the living God (10:31). Again, to echo the sentiment of the third warning, we have the assurance of forgiveness. The Christian who sins is not the same as one who utterly rejects the Word of God once they have been enlightened. Christians who miss the mark desire forgiveness. Those who reject Christ and His offer of grace and salvation do not desire to seek repentance.

As a word of caution, Christians who deliberately and repeatedly sin because they believe forgiveness is available are marks of immaturity. And to continue to do so is to be no better than those who entirely reject God's Word out of unbelief. The writer's warning couldn't be any more explicit - "let us draw near with a true heart in full assurance of faith, with our hearts sprinkled clean from an evil conscience, and our bodies washed with pure water" (10:22). Those who live a life of purity are those who possess a full assurance of faith.

Warning Four: Despising the Word of God (10:26-29)

Rejection of Jesus Christ can be described as what?

____

____

____

Can someone accidentally blaspheme? Why not?

____

____

____

A Christian who sins is not the same as one who utterly rejects the Word of God. What is the difference?

____

____

____

Jesus the Superior Priest Notes

SECTION THREE:
JESUS THE SUPERIOR PRINCIPLE (HEBREWS 11-13)

Superior Faith (11:1-40)

Superior Endurance (12:1-29)

Exhortations and Conclusion (13:1-25)

Superior Faith (11:1-40)

The eleventh chapter of Hebrews has been called the Hall of Faith, for it includes several Old Testament heroes of the faith. The writer included these snapshots of faith intentionally. Therefore, it is necessary to remind ourselves of the context of this portion of the sermon letter.

Bookending Hebrews eleven are two essential points. First, the writer said in chapter ten: "For you have need of endurance, so that when you have done the will of God, you may receive what is promised" (10:36). Next, in chapter twelve, the writer said, "Therefore, since so great a cloud of witnesses surrounds us, let us also lay aside every weight, and sin which clings so closely, and let us run with endurance the race that is set before us" (12:1). To appeal for his audience to endure the race of faith, he expounds on several Old Testament figures who exemplified living by faith. In essence, these believers were running out of spiritual breath, and they needed endurance.

The examples include men and women who endured some of the most difficult, horrific, and terrifying times. Faith sustained these people of God, and their example should inspire Christians to also endure through faith.

Keep in mind, though these were people of faith, they were also people of failure. God calls us to faithfulness, not to perfection. Enshrined in this Hall of Faith are men and women who were not perfect. Noah got drunk after the flood. Abraham lied on a few occasions and had an illegitimate child with Hagar. Jacob deceived his father to steal his brother's birthright. Moses killed an Egyptian and even missed out on the Promised Land due to public unbelief. Samson was a womanizer. David committed adultery and murder.

Despite their hang-ups and failures, they endured. Even though they faced difficult circumstances, they persevered. The writer intended to use people of faith and failures to appeal to his audience's faith. Faith, as you see in these Old Testament saints, isn't a life of pristine purity. Instead, it's clinging to God and believing that He is better, even when you fail or face painful conditions and hardships.

Additionally, the Hall of Faith includes those who didn't escape tribulation. The writer included those tortured, mocked, flogged, imprisoned, stoned, sawn in two, and killed with the sword. They went about in skins of sheep and goats, destitute, afflicted, and mistreated. Some wandered about in deserts, mountains, dens, and caves (10:35b-38). On the other hand, some conquered kingdoms, enforced justice, obtained promises, stopped the mouths of lions, quenched the power of fire, escaped the edge of the sword, put armies to flight, and women received their loved ones back from death (10:33-35a).

Our faith doesn't decide whether we are going to be prosperous or persecuted. For instance, some escaped the edge of the sword; others were killed with a sword. Some lived in palaces and experienced great wealth and prosperity, while others lived in caves destitute and penniless. Some were draped with robes of purple, while others were clothed with skins of goats and sheep. It's not that one group had faith, and the other lacked faith. Instead, it was the same robust faith that caused them to endure all circumstances.

The prosperity gospel of today would tell you those who suffered or those who didn't receive their promises lacked faith. That's not what the writer of Hebrews records. Both groups of people endured through faith. The writer said, "And all these, though commended through their faith, did not receive what was promised." In other words, they all persevered. Yet, none of them had what New Testament believers possess - the Superior Christ!

Superior Faith Study Guide (11:1-40)

What has the eleventh chapter of Hebrews been called?

____

____

____

What is the writer trying to communicate to his readers with this record of Old Testament hero's exploits?

____

____

____

God calls us to faith and perfection. True or false?

____

____

____

Some Old Testament saints suffered fatal persecution. Was their faith deficient? On the other hand, some Old Testament saints escaped fatal persecution. Was their faith better than those killed? Explain your answer from Hebrews 11.

____

____

____

Superior Endurance (12:1-29)

"Therefore, since we are surrounded by so great a cloud of witnesses, let us also lay aside every weight, and sin which clings so closely, and let us run with endurance the race that is set before us" (12:1). The heroes of the faith serve as a cloud of witnesses proving the Hebrews can make it. While they had great faith, Jesus provided a superior principle of faith.

The Old Testament heroes didn't have Christ in His fullness. They didn't have the assistance of the Holy Spirit. Yet, they endured! Beloved, Jesus is the Author and Finisher of our faith.

Though Old Testament heroes are worthy examples of faith, the greatest of Saints is Jesus Christ: "looking to Jesus, the founder and perfecter of our faith, who for the joy that was set before him endured the cross, despising the shame, and is seated at the right hand of the throne of God. Consider him who endured from sinners such hostility against himself, so that you may not grow weary or fainthearted" (12:3). Jesus provides an even more excellent example of endurance: He endured the cross and endured hostility.

The Hebrews were exhausted and worn out. They needed strength and endurance to continue despite less-than-ideal circumstances. They needed to lay aside every weight and sin that could easily entangle them (12:1). To run with every ounce of energy requires believers to strip off anything that would burden effort. Too many ask questions like "can I do this?" or "can I do that?" or "what harm will this do to me?" When they should be asking, "Will this help me run?" If believers ask that question, they will know whether or not something is hindering or helping their race of faith.

According to the writer, endurance includes embracing the discipline of the Lord (12:5-7). Often the testing of one's faith is the discipline of God. God's discipline is to perfect a believer's character and faith. Discipline isn't evidence of God's displeasure; instead, it's proof of God's love. God disciplines those who are His children. Parents disciplining their children is for their betterment to improve upon their character (10:9). Indeed, God loves unconditionally; He loves us so much that He refuses to leave us in the condition He found us. In other words, children grow into adults, and Christians mature in their faith. Therefore, it is necessary for God and parents alike to utilize discipline to improve them.

Like the Hebrews, believers today are to embrace the hardship they might face and not abandon Christ. Difficult circumstances can be seen as the loving hand of Christ bringing about the transformation of character and faith.

Four Ethics of Those Who Endure (12:14-16)

1. Pursue peace
2. Pursue holiness
3. Pursue goodwill
4. Pursue purity

After this enduring chapter, the writer again addresses those who want to revert to the old Mosaic covenant. He uses two familiar mountains to illustrate his message. Mount Sinai represents the Law, and Mount Zion represents the New Covenant. The event of Moses receiving the Law on Mount Sinai was terrifying and invoked fear in the people. The writer contrasts that to the coronation of the heavenly Jerusalem (Mount Zion), where there will be rejoicing and jubilation in the Kingdom Age.

Superior Endurance Study Guide (12:1-29)

Who is the greatest example of faithful endurance?

____

____

____

Instead of asking questions like: "Is this a sin?" or "Will this send me to hell?" What should believers ask?

____

____

____

God's discipline is to perfect what two things?

____

____

____

Warning Five: Denying the Word of God (12:25-29)

The writer's final warning is a caution not to deny the Word of God. "See that you do not refuse him who is speaking. For if they did not escape when they refused him who warned them on earth, much less will we escape if we reject him who warns from heaven" (12:25).

The Greek word for "refuse" can be defined as "deny," "shun," or "avoid." The writer once more alludes to Israelite's who refused to listen and obey the Law of Moses. If those who denied the Word of God did not escape God's judgment, how can those who have heard the voice of Jesus Christ through the gospel of grace? The answer is obvious - they can't.

The New Covenant, which is the ultimate fulfillment of the Law of Moses, is God's final Word. Jesus Christ is God's concluding message, and God will judge humanity based upon this Word. Returning to Judaism would be useless. Looking for some other "word" or some alternate "message" is futile.

Warning Five: Denying the Word of God Study Guide (12:25-29)

The writer warns his audience not to refuse Him who is speaking. Define the word "refuse" from the Greek.

____

____

____

The writer is tying up his argument that God has spoken. God's final word is Jesus Christ. Where can one turn if they refuse Jesus Christ?

____

____

____

What is the danger of shunning Jesus Christ, God's concluding Word?

____

____

____

Exhortations and Conclusion (13:1-25)

The conclusion of the Hebrews letter is a call to practical Christian living. God's Word isn't a compilation of theoretical platitudes. Instead, God's Word is useful and suitable for application. The writer concludes his sermon letter with a call to action. He offers six virtues of the Christian life.

Six Virtues of the Christian Life

1. Brotherly love (13:1)
2. Hospitality (13:2)
3. Service of the mistreated (13:3)
4. Purity in marriage (13:4)
5. Contentment (13:5-6)
6. Submitting to Christian leadership (13:7)

Love is the outflow of being in the New Covenant. Brotherly love is to continue, which means it should already be active. The Apostle John wrote, "We know that we have passed out of death into life because we love the brothers. Whoever does not love abides in death" (1 Jn. 3:14). How can we display love to a lost world if we can't show love to one another? Some would rather forsake loving the world altogether, only to keep their small Christian circle intact. The commission of the church is to love all. Love strangers (1:2), love those who are mistreated (1:3) and love their spouses (1:3). A lack of love in any of these categories is a deficient virtue of the Christian life.

The writer gives one last but brief caution: "Jesus Christ is the same yesterday and today and forever. Do not be led away by diverse and strange teachings, for it is good for the heart to be strengthened by grace, not by foods, which have not benefited those devoted to them" (13:8-9).

Jesus Christ is the same yesterday, today, and forever. This reality is a concise summary of the writer's argument. Jesus is superior to Israel's heroes of yesterday. He is superior to Israel's ceremonial rites of yesterday. He is superior to Israel's Old Covenant of yesterday. To forsake Jesus Christ is to be carried away with strange teachings. This caution echoes Paul's arguments in Colossians (Col. 2:8-12; 3:15-23). Believers should reject those who attempt to lead believers under specific Old Testament commands regarding sacrifices, foods, and strict aestheticism. Such requirements are unprofitable for believers in Jesus Christ. He is far superior and provides a far superior sacrifice. Believers are no longer required to offer sacrifices of animals; instead, they offer the sacrifice of praisc to God continually (13:15). God is pleased with the fruit of our lips, which is praise and worship flowing from a transformed heart.

The believer's altar isn't a physical monument covered with the carcasses of animals. Instead, our altar is the superior altar of Jesus Christ (13:10-12). Christ's altar grants access to eternal benefits, which the altars of the Old Testament and various other religions could not offer. To forsake the life-giving sacrifice of Jesus Christ is to cling to that which is meaningless.

In other words, may the God of peace, who brought up from the dead our Lord Jesus, the great Shepherd of the sheep, and ratified an eternal covenant with his blood, may He equip you with all you need for doing his will. May he produce in you, through the power of Jesus Christ, every good thing that is pleasing to him. All glory to him forever and ever! Amen (13:19-20).

Exhortations and Conclusion Study Guide (13:1-25)

What are the six virtues of the Christian life?

The writer tells his audience to let brotherly love continue. Besides loving other Christians, who are believers called to love?

What sacrifice are believers to offer today?

Jesus the Superior Principle Notes

The King's Bread and Wine: **Jesus is Greater Than Melchizedek**

Everyone likes a good mystery. The essential parts of a good mystery include clues, questions, answers, speculation, and solutions. Mystery envelops the Bible character Melchizedek. He appears out of nowhere and suddenly disappears. Was he a real person? Was his appearance to Abraham a theophany (an appearance of Jesus in the O.T.)?

Part of the mystery surrounding Melchizedek is due to the writer of Hebrews statement: "He is without father or mother or genealogy, having neither beginning of days nor end of life, but resembling the Son of God he continues a priest forever" (Hebrews 7:3).

What does that mean? How does one not have a mother or father? No beginning of days? No end of life? Who is this mysterious man?

While I believe Melchizedek was a real person, despite his similar characteristics of Jesus, I do not think that he was simply a theophany. His cameo in Genesis, however, is packed with significance and worthy of our study.

History of Melchizedek

In Genesis 14, a dispute among several kings resulted in a war in the Jordan Valley, where Lot, Abraham's nephew, was living in Sodom. A coalition of kings invaded Sodom and the surrounding areas, taking Lot captive (Gen. 14:1-12). One person escaped and told Abraham of the news. Abraham gathered his trained men and went to battle with the kings who invaded Sodom, freeing Lot and recovering the cities (Gen. 14:13-16).

The king of Sodom, and Melchizedek, king of Salem, met Abraham at his return home. Time and space don't permit us to spend time on the king of Sodom here. The meeting of Melchizedek and Abraham is amazing. Abraham, the man of faith, and Melchizedek. We are intrigued when great men and women meet each other. Think of Winston Churchill and Franklin D. Roosevelt. I would have liked to have been a fly on the wall at those meetings and encounters.

The meaningful life of Abraham is essential throughout the rest of Genesis and Scripture. Melchizedek's life is briefly mentioned here. Though given a short introduction, he will be important a thousand years later when the psalmist says: "The Lord has sworn and will not change his mind, "You are a priest forever after the order of Melchizedek" (Psalm 110:4). Psalm 110 is the most quoted chapter of Psalms in the New Testament. Then another thousand years after Psalm 110 was written, the writer of Hebrews said:

"See how great this man was to whom Abraham the patriarch gave a tenth of the spoils" (Hebrews 7:4).

While much of Abraham's life of faith is recorded and recounted on throughout the Bible, Melchizedek has a small cameo and makes a giant impact.

Melchizedek: A Man of Faith and Righteousness

Scripture says Melchizedek was a priest of the most high God (Gen. 14:18). This detail is significant for a few reasons. First, he was a servant of the Lord in a rather godless region. The people of the Jordan Valley were anything but worshipers of Jehovah. For Melchizedek to be considered godly at this time, and in this place, gives us reason to believe he was a man of faith. People who live contrary to their surrounding culture are considered to be counter-cultural. Melchizedek was a man of faith in a faithless world. If you are going to impact the world, you must not be like the world. We don't know where Melchizedek learned about the Lord. The details of his conversion aren't given. What we do know is that he was righteous, for Paul said, "The righteous live by faith" (Rom. 1:17).

The writer of Hebrews said Melchizedek's name meant "king of righteousness" (Heb. 7:2). Righteousness means to live according to God's law. Melchizedek lived by a higher law than that of his surrounding people. One writer said, "Righteousness exalts a nation, but sin condemns any people" (Pro. 14:34).

Do you see the first connection between Melchizedek and Jesus? Jesus is the King of Righteousness. He is superior to Melchizedek because the righteousness of humanity is as filthy rags (Isa. 64:6). We cannot claim our righteousness as any good. What righteousness we have has been attributed to us from the perfect righteousness of Jesus Christ. Jesus perfectly obeyed the Word of God:

"Although he was a son, he learned obedience through what he suffered. And being made perfect, he became the source of eternal salvation to all who obey him" (Heb. 5:8–9). Through Christ's perfect obedience, He took our sin, and gave us His righteousness (2 Cor. 5:21; Rom. 3:21-22; 4:6, 11; 5:18-19).

A Priest and King

The second interesting reason to Melchizedek's priesthood is that he is not from the Levitical priesthood. Levi hadn't been born yet, and the Mosaic Law was about 500 years in the future. This information is significant because Melchizedek's priesthood was not based upon lineage or inheritance, much like Jesus. The writer of Hebrews draws this conclusion:

"Now if perfection had been attainable through the Levitical priesthood (for under it the people received the law), what further need would there have been for another priest to arise after the order of Melchizedek, rather than one named after the order of Aaron? For when there is a change in the priesthood, there is necessarily a change in the law as well. For the one of whom these things are spoken belonged to another tribe, from which no one has ever served at the altar. For it is evident that our Lord was descended from Judah, and in connection with that tribe Moses said nothing about priests. This becomes even more evident when another priest arises in the likeness of Melchizedek, who has become a priest, not on the basis of a legal requirement concerning bodily descent, but by the power of an indestructible life. For it is witnessed of him, 'You are a priest forever, after the order of Melchizedek.' For on the one hand, a former commandment is set aside because of its weakness and uselessness" (Heb. 7:11-18)

Jesus came as a priest after the order of Melchizedek forever. The point isn't that Melchizedek didn't have a mother or father, it's that no record was given. Therefore, after the similitude of one who seems to be "forever," Jesus is a priest for all of eternity. The Levitical priesthood was only to be temporary. The sacrifices they made were never going to be sufficient to remove the sins of all of humanity. The blood of bulls and goats would not wash away sins. Part of this insufficiency was that the Levitical priests were human and would die (Heb. 7:23). Jesus is superior to the Levitical priesthood and the Melchizedekian priesthood because He lives forever (Heb. 7:15-16).

Moreover, Melchizedek was said to be King of Salem and a priest of the most high God. Israel's priesthood began with Aaron and was passed down through his descendants (from the tribe of Levi). When Israel's kingship arose a few centuries later, the monarchy and priesthood were kept separate. No one could simultaneously be king and priest. King Uzziah attempted to do priestly tasks, and God struck him with leprosy (2 Chron. 26:16–21). Melchizedek predates the Levitical priesthood and the monarchy of Israel. Again, this points us to Jesus. He is both King and High Priest.

As King, He is the Creator ruling and governing. As Priest He represents God to us and represents us to God. This is important because Jesus is in heaven right now, interceding on our behalf (Heb. 7:25).

"*If I can hear Christ praying for me in the next room, I would not fear a million enemies. Yet the distance makes no difference; He is praying for me*" - Robert M'Cheyne

Jesus, as our High Priest, is praying for us. Did you fail to pray today? Jesus didn't miss the prayer meeting. Beloved, rest in this reality that Jesus is praying for you right now.

Notice as well, Melchizedek is said to be king of Salem. Salem was the location of Jerusalem. "*Jeru*" was added years later to the name "*Salem,*" making the name Jerusalem. Psalm 76:2 makes this Salem to be Jerusalem, "In Salem also is his tabernacle and his dwelling place in Zion."

The word "*Salem*" in Hebrew means "*peace*" or "*complete.*" It is where the word Shalom derives. Melchizedek is king of peace, and his name means righteousness. The writer of Hebrews wrote, "to whom also Abraham gave a tenth part of all; first being by interpretation King of righteousness, and after that also King of Salem, which is, King of peace" (Hebrews 7:2). The truth taught here is that righteousness comes before peace. The world needs to be taught this truth. People everywhere want peace, but peace follows righteousness. The prophet Isaiah said, "And the work of righteousness shall be peace, and the effect of righteousness quietness and assurance forever" (Isa. 32:17). Jesus is the King of Righteousness. He perfectly obeyed and fulfilled the Law of Moses on our behalf.

Jesus is far superior because He is King of Peace. The Bible speaks of peace in two different ways. There is subjective peace, and there is objective peace. Subjective peace is peace within your mind and emotions. It's a tranquility of the mind, or a positive feeling of safety. This is the peace of God in our hearts. It's the assurance of knowing that a sovereign God is in control.

Objective peace, on the other hand, is quite different. Paul writes, "Therefore being justified by faith, we have peace with God through our Lord Jesus Christ" (Rom. 5:1). This is not the peace *of* God; rather, this is peace *with* God. This concerns our relationship with God. And thus, it implies that we were once at war with God. Romans 5:10 says, "For if, when we were enemies, we were reconciled to God by the death of his Son, much more, being reconciled, we shall be saved by his life." Put another way, our sin kept us at war with God.

But God shows His love for us in that while we were sinners, Christ died for us. Jesus, the King of Righteousness, brought about peace. Another writer said it like this: "Mercy and truth are met together; Righteousness and peace have kissed each other" (Psalm 85:10).

Thank God that Jesus is both King of Righteousness and King of Peace. He is King of kings. He is also the merciful and faithful High Priest in things pertaining to God, to make reconciliation for the sins of the people (Heb. 2:17).

The King's Bread and Wine

Let's return to Genesis 14 to see even more.

"And Melchizedek king of Salem brought out bread and wine. (He was priest of God Most High.) And he blessed him and said, 'Blessed be Abram by God Most High, Possessor of heaven and earth; and blessed be God Most High, who has delivered your enemies into your hand!'

And Abram gave him a tenth of everything" (Gen. 14:18-20).

Melchizedek meets Abraham and brings him bread and wine. The King-Priest of Salem comes bearing gifts for a weary man. Abraham has just returned from the battle. He is depleted and exhausted. Suddenly a mysterious man comes to bring Abraham bread and wine. Abraham, a man of faith, following the promises of God, needed replenishment. He had just fought a battle and needed a little encouragement. So the King-Priest blessed a faithful and worn-out man with bread and wine.

Beloved, do you see how Melchizedek prefigures Jesus Christ? Again, the writer of Hebrews wrote this: "For the moment all discipline seems painful rather than pleasant, but later it yields the peaceful fruit of righteousness to those who have been trained by it. Therefore lift your drooping hands and strengthen your weak knees, and make straight paths for your feet, so that what is lame may not be put out of joint but rather be healed. Strive for peace with everyone, and for the holiness without which no one will see the Lord" (Heb. 12:11-14).

What will give you life? What will replenish your soul? What will yield righteousness and peace?

The writer of Hebrews tells us and connects us back to Jesus:

"Consequently, when Christ came into the world, he said, "Sacrifices and offerings you have not desired, but a body have you prepared for me; in burnt offerings and sin offerings you have taken no pleasure. Then I said, 'Behold, I have come to do your will, O God, as it is written of me in the scroll of the book.' When he said above, 'You have neither desired nor taken pleasure in sacrifices and offerings and burnt offerings and sin offerings' (these are offered according to the law), then he added, 'Behold, I have come to do your will.' He does away with the first in order to establish the second. And by that will we have been sanctified through the offering of the body of Jesus Christ once for all" (Heb. 10:5-10).

Do you see it yet?

"Now as they were eating, Jesus took bread, and after blessing it broke it and gave it to the disciples, and said, 'Take, eat; this is my body.' And he took a cup, and when he had given thanks he gave it to them, saying, 'Drink of it, all of you, for this is my blood of the covenant, which is poured out for many for the forgiveness of sins. I tell you I will not drink again of this fruit of the vine until that day when I drink it new with you in my Father's kingdom'" (Matt. 26:26-29).

Jesus is far superior to Melchizedek because He is the only King-Priest who gives us his body as life-giving bread and his blood, as soul-cleansing wine. Jesus, our King-Priest, is the Ancient of Days. He is the beginning and the ending. He is the Rock of Ages, able to reign and represent God to us and us to God forever.

Are you weary of fighting against God's call? Come and partake of the King's bread and wine. Do you need peace with God? Come and eat the King's bread and wine. Do you need a righteousness that only comes from God? Then come and partake of the King's bread and wine. Do you need cleansing? Then partake of the King's bread and wine.

The King's Bread and Wine Notes

The Tabernacle of God

It had been an interesting few days for the Israelites. Jehovah had just liberated them from Egypt's fetters as His might and power were on display in the plagues and parting of the Red Sea. They traveled to Mount Sinai, where Moses, who had led them out of Egypt, would meet with God face to face. The Lord of Hosts was going to give Moses and Israel a plan. Now that they were free from the chains of Egypt, they needed to be free from the bondage of sin. They were out of Egypt, but now they needed to get Egypt out of them. Liberation came with a price and a new lifestyle. Here at Mount Sinai, they would be given the Law. Besides the commandments written on tablets of stone, Jehovah gave Moses a divine plan. God was going to dwell among His chosen people.

And let them make me a sanctuary, that I may dwell in their midst. Exactly as I show you concerning the pattern of the Tabernacle, and of all its furniture, so you shall make it (Exodus 25:8–9).

The Tabernacle in the Wilderness would serve as a type and shadow of heavenly realities.

They serve as a copy and shadow of the heavenly things. For when Moses was about to erect the tent, he was instructed by God, saying, "See that you make everything according to the pattern that was shown you on the mountain" (Hebrews 8:5).

If God was going dwell among His people, then there needed to be a blueprint. The world has never seen a perfect structure other than the Tabernacle, for He was the Divine architect. Every detail was given attention and was baptized with meaning. This was the blueprint, and it was to be followed correctly. This transportable sacred structure would only be stationary at particular points in the Wilderness. When they set up the Tabernacle, it would dwell at the center of the camp, with each tribe strategically situated. The presence of God was to be the center of the Israelite's life as they wandered the Wilderness.

Much could be written about the Tabernacle in the Wilderness, for it is teeming with spiritual significance. Please note we have only two chapters in Scripture concerning the creation, but we have close to fifty chapters concerning the Tabernacle. God would rather us be more attentive to His dwelling among His people.

The Perfect Pattern

When the Lord began to give Moses the pattern for the Tabernacle, He started with the interior and worked his way out. The blueprint started in the holy of holies with the Ark of the Covenant and worked inside to outside. So it is with the Christian. Salvation begins in the inner man in his heart, and then sanctification works inside out. For our brief survey, we are going to work through the Tabernacle as it would be approached.

Located in the courtyard and within the Tabernacle, structure would be objects and furnishings which would serve in the worship of the inhabiting presence of Jehovah. Each item would perform a particular function.

- The Brazen Altar
- The Laver
- The Table of Showbread
- The Golden Lamp Stand
- The Altar of Incense
- The Ark of the Covenant and Mercy Seat

The Altar

The Tabernacle would be surrounded with linen curtains serving as a fence. The purpose of this fence was to keep men out. The curtains stood seven and a half feet tall; bystanders could not casually see what was happening in the courts of the Tabernacle; they would have to come in. Anyone could come, but you must enter by the one entrance. One could not jump over the fence or slide under the fence. No, there was only one entrance. The one entrance was embroidered with blue, scarlet, and purple needlework (Ex. 38:18).

Once you entered the door and entered the court of the Tabernacle, the Brazen Altar met you. The Altar for burnt offerings stood just inside the door. It was the shape of a square, measuring seven and a half feet long and wide and four and a half feet high. It was large and could support the sacrifice of lambs, bulls, and oxen. This was the largest piece of equipment. Built of wood and overlaid with brass, here the sacrifice was slain and burned. However, no man started the fire, the fire was kindled from heaven, and it was never to go out (Lev. 6:12-13; 9:24). Salvation is of the Lord, and His fire never goes out!

The Laver

The Laver was made of solid brass and was to be filled with pure water (Ex. 30:17-21; 38:8). The priests would wash their hands and feet after stopping at the Altar. The Laver is representative of our washing and cleansing. And this can only come after the burnt offering. To be born again and washed in pure water for the remission of our sins can only come after spiritual death at repentance.

One should note that the size of the Laver is never mentioned, whereas all the other dimensions and details for all other furnishings are given. But the Laver size is not given, perhaps because any and all can be washed. The Altar was large enough to kill the sacrifice, but the Laver was large enough to cleanse the vilest of sinners. It was limitless in its function. With no floor in the Tabernacle or the court, the priest's feet constantly contact the ground. Oh, for washing and a cleansing! There must be continual washing for the Christian. Sins could be forgiven, but the defilements of the world need remission. To be made new and washed clean!

The Table of Showbread

Once you are washed at the Laver you enter the Holy Place. The sacrifice has been accepted, the water has washed away the defilements, and you can now enter fellowship.

Three pieces of furniture were in the Holy Place, the table of showbread, the golden lampstand, and the Altar of incense.

On the north side of the Holy Place was the table of showbread. The table was made of acacia wood and overlaid with pure gold. The table's dimensions were three feet long, one and half feet wide, and two and a quarter feet high (Ex. 25:23-24). The table also had parts to which it could be easily transported, including its utensils (Ex. 25:24-29). Each week, twelve pieces of bread would be placed on the table–two stacks of six loaves. The bread was not food for God, like some pagan god. Instead, this represented God's people being physically sustained by Jehovah. This bread was to be eaten by the priests. The bread was representative of the Word of God to be eaten and digested.

The Golden Lamp Stand

Across from the table of showbread was thc Golden Lamp Stand or Candlestick (Ex. 25:31-40). It was made of beaten pure gold. There were seven branches, three standing on each side and one in the middle. In the outer court of the Tabernacle, the light would be provided by the sun. However, in the Holy Place, the light illuminated from the golden candlestick. There were no windows or electricity, only the candlestick. The oil provided the light, which was made of pure beaten olive oil. The fresh oil from the unripened olives would give a smokeless light. The people would provide the oil for the illumination in the Holy Place. The bread was eaten under the illumination of the oil-sustained candlestick.

The Altar of Incense

Standing in front of the veil of the Holy of Holies was the Altar of Incense. The Golden Candlestick is glowing, the bread has been eaten, and now the High Priest draws near the Altar of Incense. Before he can go into the holiest place, he must come to the place of prayer. It was made of wood and overlaid with pure gold. It stood three feet high and one-half feet square. It sat at the central position in the Holy Place, between the Table of Showbread and the Golden Candlestick. Every morning Aaron the High Priest was to burn incense upon it.

Prayer is necessary for fellowship with God. We partake of His Word, our hearts and minds are illuminated by His guiding light, and we commune with Him in prayer. Here at the Altar of Incense, we send up our supplications and intercessions. It is a sweet-smelling aroma unto the Lord.

The Holy of Holies

Now the priest enters the Holy of Holies through the veil directly behind the Altar of incense. Here, in the holiest place, stood the Ark of the Covenant and Mercy Seat. This was the most important piece of the Tabernacle. The Holy of Holies was fifteen feet high, wide, and long. It was separated from the Holy Place by a heavy curtain or veil.

The Ark of the Covenant was three and three-fourths feet long, two and one-fourth feet wide, and two and one-fourth feet high. It was made of wood, covered with gold. The Ark contained the written Law, a pot of manna, and Aaron's rod that budded. Sitting on top of the Ark was the golden mercy seat with two cherubim with their outstretched wings touching.

The Ark was a symbol of God's throne. On the Day of Atonement, the High Priest would enter this last room and sprinkle blood on the Mercy Seat from the slain sacrifice. The broken Law housed in the Ark needed a mercy seat and shed blood to cover it. But it was here, at the Ark of the Covenant in the Holy of Holies, that the Shekinah Glory of God would hover. The glory of God would dwell where the shed blood of redemption was applied. The broken Law is covered by mercy and blood. The Spirit of God would not stay where the blood wasn't applied.

Once the Tabernacle was completed and erected, the glory of the Lord filled the Tabernacle (Ex. 40:34-35). Moses was unable to enter the Tabernacle due to the Spirit of God richly dwelling there.

The New Testament Tabernacle of God

Now, we must understand the significance of the Tabernacle in the New Testament. The writer of Hebrews stated that the Tabernacle was a shadow and copy of heavenly realities. But the Tabernacle in the Wilderness was only temporary. It could not and would not last forever, and it would begin to deteriorate with time and the elements. The sacrifices proved to be insufficient for man's sins. God would only be at one location on earth at the Tabernacle, though His Spirit is omnipresent. If God was going to dwell among His people, then another tabernacle was needed.

John's Gospel is significant, for he pens his opening declaring that Jesus Christ is the Word of God dwelling among us (Jn. 1:1-3, 14). He uses the phrase "dwelt among us" to describe the Living Word of God as coming to earth. The word "dwelt" in the original language means to "pitch a tent."

The Tabernacle was the dwelling-place of Jehovah, the meeting-place of God and Israel. So the Word came to men in the person of Jesus. Jehovah adopted a dwelling for His habitation like that of the people in the Wilderness. The Word assumed a community of nature with humanity, an embodiment like humanity at large, and became flesh.

There is also a fascinating parallel between the structure of John's Gospel and the Tabernacle of the Old Testament.

The Tabernacle in the Wilderness was in three parts: The courtyard, the holy place, and the holy of holies. But it should be noted that it was only one Tabernacle. There may have been three different areas of that one Tabernacle, but it was still one Tabernacle. The Ark of the Covenant standing in the holy of holies was wood covered in gold on both the inside and outside. Three parts - gold (divine), wood (humanity), gold (divine). Again, only one Ark of the Covenant. The Tabernacle and the Ark of the Covenant are a shadow of heavenly things but represent Jesus Christ in reality. Jesus was Tabernacled among us. Not many could understand that Jesus was the embodiment of God the Father. He was Father (divine), Son (humanity), and Spirit (divine).

The Tabernacle in the Wilderness was furnished with seven significant pieces that pointed to Jesus Christ. When we come to John's Gospel, we find those same seven furnishings in the same order. Whether or not John purposed this or not, or whether He was divinely inspired to categorize these things in this way, is not certain. However, we should note that everything was done according to pattern (Heb. 8:5).

The New Testament Altar

John begins by saying that Jesus Christ was "tabernacled" among us (Jn. 1:14). But it is John the Baptist who points to the Brazen Altar and declares Jesus to be the Lamb of God come to take away the sins of the world (Jn. 1:29). It will be Jesus' death at Calvary that will bring atonement for the sins of the world. Jesus as the Lamb of God will once and for all end the necessity for sacrifice (Heb 8:13).

The New Testament Laver

Next, in the third chapter of John's Gospel, we find Jesus taking us to the Laver. When Nicodemus, a learned Jewish rabbi, comes at night to speak with the Lord, Jesus tells him that you must be born again of the water and the Spirit, or you cannot see or enter the Kingdom of God (Jn. 3:3-6). You must be washed and sanctified by the water. It is not enough to have the Lamb of God on the Altar; you must be washed.

The New Testament Table of Showbread

Following the Laver, we find in John chapter four, five, and six that John takes us to the table of showbread. Jesus tells the woman at the well that He is the Living water, of which if a man drinks, he shall never thirst again (Jn. 4:10; 13-14). He tells His disciples that His food is to do the will of Him who sent Him (Jn. 5:34). In John five, Jesus tells his audience that the life-giving Scriptures speak of Him (Jn. 5:39). Then Jesus explains that He is the bread of life, that if a man comes to Him, he will never hunger again (Jn. 6:25). Jesus was the bread come down from heaven, and whoever eats on this bread will live forever (Jn. 6:57-58). Many turned from following Him at this saying, but Peter knew that Jesus was the Word of eternal life.

The New Testament Golden Lamp Stand

Next, in John chapter eight, John walks us to the Golden Lamp Stand. Jesus declares that He is the Light of the World and that whoever follows Him will not walk in darkness but will have the light of life. In Jesus was life, and the life was the light of men. The light shines in darkness, and darkness will not overcome it (Jn. 1:4-5).

Jesus' light brings sight to the blind, but those who do not believe remain blind in their darkness (Jn. 9:39-41).

The New Testament Altar of Incense

Then in John, chapters fourteen through seventeen, we see Jesus with the eleven teaching them to pray at the Altar of Incense. He teaches them to pray at the golden Altar in a way and through a Name unknown before. Previously the priest stood at the Altar of Incense offering prayers for Israel. Now, Jesus is showing that prayer in His Name is the way of intercession and supplication. That powerful Name in prayer hadn't been known before. If they would abide in Jesus and His words, they could ask whatever they desired and it would be done for them (Jn. 15:7). However, now His Name had been manifested, and faith in that name brought power to prayers. But in that High Priestly prayer in John seventeen, we see Jesus, our High Priest, offering supplications and intercession for His disciples at the Golden Altar of Incense.

The New Testament Ark of the Covenant and Shekinah Glory

Finally, in the climax of Calvary in John eighteen and nineteen, we see the Ark of the Covenant and the Mercy Seat. Jesus is the very Ark of the Covenant, and its Mercy Seat sprinkled with His blood. The sins of the world had been atoned for, and the Law which had been broken was now covered with the blood of Jesus Christ.

Instead of a broken covenant with God the Father, we have a new covenant through the death and resurrection of Jesus Christ in which He says, "I am ascending to my Father and your Father, to my God, and your God" (Jn. 20:17).

However, once the blood had sprinkled on the Ark of the Covenant and everything was finished, the glory of God would fill the Tabernacle with the Shekinah Glory. This is the new Shekinah glory! And here, John shows us that it is the gift of the Holy Spirit, that now fills our earthen vessel, "And when he had said this, he breathed on them and said to them, 'Receive ye the Holy Ghost'" (Jn. 20:22).

Brothers and sisters, the Tabernacle in the Old Testament was only a type and shadow of a heavenly reality. It pointed to a better tabernacle and a better dwelling. God did not want to dwell in a tent made of hands. He was the Word of God tabernacled in the flesh. He was the Lamb of God, taking away the sins of the world. He was the bread of life and the living water. He was the light shining in the darkness of sin. He has given us a Name to be used in prayer and supplication. He was the Ark of the Covenant housing the Word of God, the bread of God, and the power of God. And He was the Mercy Seat which brought grace upon grace. However, what could be better than Christ being tabernacled among us? It is expedient that He which dwelt among us go away so that He can be in us (Jn. 14:-16-17).

Behold, the Tabernacle of God!

The Tabernacle of God Notes

OTHER TITLES FROM NATHAN S. WHITLEY

The Lost Art of Spiritual Disciplines
I AM: Studies in the I AM Declarations of Jesus Christ
Five Steps to Effective Prayer

BIBLE EXPOSITION SERIES

Colossians: Christ All in All
Hebrews: Christ is Superior

For more information and resources visit:
nswhitley.com

Made in the USA
Columbia, SC
14 September 2023